Steam Memories: 1950's – 1960's

No. 44: East Coast Main Li...

David Dunn

Copyright Book Law Publications 2013

ISBN 978-1-909625-03-7

INTRODUCTION

This third instalment of our epic journey along the East Coast Main Line finds us where the second part ECML: 2 brought us to – Retford. The Nottinghamshire town was renowned in railway circles for having that famous flat crossing where the west-to-east Manchester, Sheffield & Lincolnshire Railway met on the level with the south-to-north Great Northern Railway resulting in a crossing which remained in use for more than a hundred years without major incident. Full of interest, Retford will be given a bit more time to show off its merits. From there we get to perhaps one of the most important centres of the whole journey, at least as far as ECML motive power is concerned – Doncaster. After the complex layout of Black Carr and its myriad of junctions, we come across the engine shed at Carr on the Up side of the line. From there we go to the locomotive works known locally as the 'Plant' works where most of those Pacifics working the ECML expresses were built and all of them maintained. Next is the station before we set off northwards again, this time as far as Selby.

David Dunn, Cramlington, 2013

Cover Picture

V2 No.60956 runs through the junction at Black Carr with an Up express on 19th September 1953. *Norman Preedy.*

Title Page Picture

To begin our feast of 'Streaks', and there are many in this album, we present No.60007 SIR NIGEL GRESLEY standing in platform 4 at the head of the Up working of the *THE STEPHENSON JUBILEE* on Saturday 23rd May 1959. The King's Cross A4 was immaculate and even the visible Mk.1 carriage stock looked rather smart and was probably new. It is late afternoon and many of the platform occupants are possibly passengers from the special which have come to admire their motive power prior to the return trip to London. *I.S.Carr.*

Printed and bound by The Amadeus Press, Cleckheaton, West Yorkshire

First published in the United Kingdom by Book Law Publications, 382 Carlton Hill, Nottingham, NG4 1JA

Before we move on from Retford to continue our northbound journey along the ECML, it is worth having a further look around the junction town to make sure any gems missed initially are not overlooked this time. Going to the eastern extremity of the yard at the former GCR shed located at Thrumpton on Sunday 28th September 1958, we get this nice vista from the roadway leading off London Road (the old A1) which gives an overall view of the depot and its occupants. Nearest the camera are the sidings where the shed's overflow locomotives were stabled, besides a few stored ready for works visits. Amongst the throng here are former GC, GN and LNER standard types along with a WD 2-8-0 with the usual coating of grime. The WD was obviously a visitor because Retford did not have any 'Austerities' allocated during BR days until the summer of 1961. On the extreme right of the yard, beyond the turntable, and above the young spotters' head, can be seen the roofless and ancient 15-ton capacity travelling breakdown crane entrusted to this depot. The crane dated from 1892 and was originally one of a pair supplied to the GNR by crane maker Thomas Smith of Rodley, Leeds for civil engineering use but they had become the property of the motive power department circa 1902 when Ivatt insisted on their services for breakdowns. Retford had acquired their example (No.108) from Ardsley when BR came into being and managed to keep it until the engine shed was closed. Sheerlegs dominate the centre foreground but the pair of locomotives sharing that road – a J11 and an O2 – are simply stabled for the weekend. Other locomotives are gathered at the west end of the yard besides sharing the three-road engine shed located just behind the corrugation clad coaling stage. The brick base water tank stands between the two groups of engines and is the only original feature of the depots structures, everything else having been rebuilt, renewed or replaced. In the centre background, to the right of the tall chimney, can be seen the premises of the Northern Rubber Co., which had a long tradition of railway connections including one very famous one. *N.W.Skinner.*

In April 1961, one of Retford's resident Gresley O2s, No.63983 simmers on one of the stabling roads overlooked by the residential properties of aforementioned London Road. *D.J.Dippie.*

BR Std. 9F No.92035 resides on Thrumpton shed yard during the weekend of 22nd and 23rd June 1963 and is minus a shed plate. The big engine was in fact in transit between its old home at New England and its new one at Immingham which perhaps explains the lack of plate. One aspect of this engine which stands out like a 'sore thumb' is the rather clean exterior which contradicts somewhat the prevailing conditions at New England during this period when a thick layer of filth was the norm. The reason for No.92035's relatively smart demeanour is explained by the fact that it had recently returned from a Casual Light repair at Crewe. Immingham kept hold of this engine until January 1966 when it went into store; it was condemned a month later and turned out to be one of the longest lived Eastern Region 9Fs clocking up eleven years and one month in service. In 9F terms that was a very long time! *C.J.B.Sanderson.*

In complete contrast to the 9F we present the J11 No.64287 which was stabled on Thrumpton shed yard on Sunday 18th August 1957. Coaled up and ready for Monday's toil, the 0-6-0 had been resident at Retford since December 1929 when it transferred from Lincoln. No.64287 was approaching its 56th birthday when this image was recorded but it was far from finished and would carry on working for another twenty-one months before it was called into Gorton for the final time. *D.Fairley.*

Resident O4 No.63736 stables outside the east end of the shed at Thrumpton on 23rd June 1963. The original GCR condition 2-8-0 was by now into its final year of BR service, all of which had been carried out from this depot. Withdrawal was only nine weeks away and Doncaster cut up the locomotive shortly afterwards. This view allows us to see the large number of corrugated iron sheets used to clad both the roof and walls of the coaling stage. History would put the fitting of the covering into the period immediately before, during or after the Second World War. The engine shed was fashioned from the original 1849 brick-built edifice which had been rebuilt by BR in 1949. In Part 2 of this series it was stated that the shed here consisted just two roads but in fact it consisted three roads, but only two of them ran through the western end of the building into another yard – apologies for not being more precise. Note the coaling crane inside the stage; a simple device which saved a lot of heaving and throwing for the coalmen working therein. Note, however, the quality of the load in 63736's tender; only to be expected I suppose for a depot located in the heart of the very productive Nottinghamshire/South Yorkshire coalfield. *C.J.B.Sanderson.*

Same digits, different arrangement! O4 No.63637 heads a line of withdrawn locomotives at Thrumpton on 23rd June 1963. One of the LNER 1928 purchased O4s, from the Ministry of Munitions, this 2-8-0 had also been a fairly long-term resident of Retford having arrived there from Immingham in January 1939. Constructed by Nasmyth Wilson in October 1918, it spent nearly ten years in storage before being snapped up 'for a song' by the LNER. This scene here could well be a re-enactment of one of the post WW1 storage sites but alas, No.63637 was condemned six months prior to the image being recorded on film. This 2-8-0 was, like No.63736, another which went to Doncaster for cutting up but whereas No.63736 was fed into the works the day after being condemned, No.63637 arrived at Doncaster more than a fortnight after No.63736. Still with us? Good! Because all the O2s were being 'phased out' at Retford in 1963, an equal number of WD 2-8-0 were drafted in to take their place working the final vestiges of steam hauled coal trains around the district. Evidence of the WD invasion is visible at both ends of the yard now. *C.J.B.Sanderson.*

Further evidence of the WD invasion! Not quite. No.90108 was stabled at Thrumpton shed on that 23rd day of June 1963 but it was only visiting. The Frodingham based 'Austerity' was in the usual WD livery of filth coating filth. However, it was in a mechanically healthier state than most of the engines on this yard and managed to remain operational for another two years thanks to a Heavy Intermediate overhaul at Gorton during the early summer of 1962. *C.J.B.Sanderson.*

Prior to returning to the station, this irresistible view of the yard at Thrumpton on 7th July 1963, but from another aspect, is worth study. With No.63637 still tucked away, Gresley O2 No.63971 takes centre stage but it too is amongst the withdrawn engines. Although it is a Sunday, the track gang are busy; not dismantling the roads here as might be expected, but renewing them instead, which, for a location such as an engine shed with limited life, made a nice refreshing change. I wonder why such an exercise took place? Was it a training exercise? Unlikely as Sunday overtime would make such an undertaking rather expensive. One can only surmise that with the coming of the diesels it might be prudent to give the new motive power a sure footing if they were to be stabled at this place. I wonder if the gang had a look-out? *C.J.B.Sanderson.*

Alongside the engine shed at Thrumpton ran the former GCR main line into Lincolnshire and on an unrecorded date in the early 1960s, Darnall K3 No.61907 is seen passing the shed whilst in charge of a Sheffield (Victoria)-Cleethorpes working which it appears has just restarted from a Retford stop. *P.J.Robinson.*

Back at the station, we arrive just in time to see a southbound express departing for King's Cross – some 138.41 miles away – behind Peppercorn A1 No.60117 BOIS ROUSSEL. The date is 15th March 1963, a Friday, and main line express steam working is slowly being wound down, the diesels having become entrenched now that they were over their winter hiccup. The working days of this Pacific and its ilk are indeed numbered. Note the 10 m.p.h. speed limit in force on the eastbound spur serving the Up platform as the platform follows the junction to join the west-east main line. *F.W.Hampson.*

On the same wet and miserable Friday in March 1963, Thompson B1 No.61087 runs through on the Up main with a one-coach special showing express headlamps. Goodness knows what the vehicle was, Engineers saloon?, but it appears to be of Gresley period design. Note that Retford station has now entered the modern era and has lost its totems in favour of fluorescent lighting incorporating the name within the shade. Semaphore signals still however control the routes. *F.W.Hampson.*

The sun is out now – yes it is still that Friday 15th March 1963 – but it is late afternoon and photography would soon be impossible. However, this view of the main line, looking south, reveals one of New England's BR Standard 9Fs, No.92041, approaching the flat crossing at a steady speed with a Down express freight. At this time freight traffic was still big business for the Eastern Region with minerals, bulk liquids and powders still generating a reasonable income for the region as a whole. The 9F 2-10-0s allocated to Doncaster and New England took care of much of the north-south main line freight but the WD 2-8-0s along with the dwindling numbers of Robinson O4s still moved much of the mineral traffic from the local collieries. Diesels were in the wings ready to take over all of the freight workings but before they could begin moving the mountains of coal from the collieries to the three forthcoming Trent Valley power stations located east of Retford, a new railway had to be constructed which eliminated all conflicting movements with the ECML – a dive under. It is that exact spot where the new line was to burrow beneath the ECML which we are now looking at just prior to construction starting. *F.W.Hampson.*

Heading back to Scunthorpe with another load of coke for the hungry steelworks in the town, Frodingham WD No.90161 proceeds over the flat crossing at Retford on its way east during the afternoon of 15th March 1963. These hopper trains plying between the coking plants of south Yorkshire and the steel making plants in Lincolnshire would have a brakevan attached to each end of the formation because of a necessary reversing movement which was undertaken at Wrawby junction, Barnetby. With the amount of traffic using the junction at Wrawby for reverse moves, it is a wonder that a spur from the Retford line to give direct access to the Scunthorpe area was never put in. The coke traffic along this route was considerable and some idea of the scale can be gleaned from the fact that the coking plants of south Yorkshire and north Derbyshire at this time were producing the following amounts every year, not all of it destined for steel making but nevertheless the bulk of the tonnage was: Hardwick 274,000 tons; Grassmoor 274,000 tons; Dinnington 208,000 tons; Manvers 387,000 tons; two small plants at Nunnery 390,000 tons combined; Smithywood 458,000 tons; United Coke & Chemicals at Orgreave 865,000 tons. The steelworks of Scunthorpe were also producing their own coke at this time but their combined capacity of 2,240,000 tons could not satisfy the demand of the steel process. As the 2-8-0 rumbles over the crossing the fireman cannot help but take a look along the bisecting ECML just in case something was approaching from the south; the driver was probably doing the same thing and looking northwards on the other side of the cab. Note that the cabside numbers on the 'Austerity' are in fact chalked-on over the approximate line of the original numbers. To sum up, it was no wonder that BR decided to construct that burrowing route beneath the ECML because the coal trains, along with return empties, finished steel products, and general goods trains were all requiring more and more paths over this small and very important piece of Nottinghamshire. *F.W.Hampson.*

Before we move on, a last look at that flat crossing, for which Retford was indeed famous, shows a northbound express approaching at the maximum permissible speed. The date is Sunday 12th May 1963 and the warmth of summer is not too far away. A grotty looking Peppercorn A1, No.60157 GREAT EASTERN, is the motive power but no matter, it is still steam haulage. *I.Falcus.*

The signal box which controlled the flat crossing, Retford South, shows up nicely in this view captured on a warm Saturday 4th August 1962. Commissioned in 1892, this box was taken out of use on 27th May 1965 when the dive-under was opened throughout. The open window today would enable any enthusiasts gathered on the Up platform – and there were many – to hear the bells and the crashing of levers which presaged approaching trains – magic memories which were soon to disappear. *H.Forster.*

J6 No.64236 was another 0-6-0 tender engine which had put in some years of service but no quite as much as its GC counterpart at Thrumpton. In age terms, this Gresley era GNR engine was just coming up to its 43rd birthday, most of those years spent shifting coal with the first thirty at Colwick. A change of scenery in April 1945 took it over to the seaside at Boston but after twelve months of 'r and r' it was back to the grind, this time at Doncaster. Ten years later Retford called and the Doncaster-built 0-6-0 transferred for the final time on 14th October 1956. This scene was recorded on Sunday 18th August 1957 when No.64236 had nearly four years of active life still ahead of it. A forthcoming General overhaul would no doubt help the 0-6-0 achieve its forty-seven years of service before retirement in April 1961. In case you are wondering, the V2 front end belongs to No.60842 of Grantham. *D.Fairley.*

Another glimpse in the yard of the former Great Northern engine shed, this one back in the mid-1950s reveals this view of A4 No.60022 MALLARD. The presence of the Pacific conjures up all sorts of assumptions as to why it was there: Failed whilst working a southbound express; likewise whilst on a test run from Doncaster works; and so on! For whatever the reason, it was not an everyday occurrence to find one of Gresley's finest on the shed yard at this place. Of course an exact date would help in some way but that is not forthcoming. Nevertheless, as it's our final image at Retford, it makes a nice change from the usual O2, O4, J6, B1 offerings normally on view at this depot. *K.H.Cockerill.*

Heading north along the main line now we meet Peppercorn A1 No.60141 ABBOTSFORD as it approaches Retford from its Doncaster stop with the Up *YORKSHIRE PULLMAN* on 27th June 1961. With 'eleven on', this was a heavy load but well within the capabilities of this Copley Hill Pacific. *R.H.Leslie.*

Exactly a week beforehand, and at near enough the same location, V2 No.60902 passed by with a southbound freight as we eat our sandwiches by the gradient post. The date is 20th June 1961. A rather dull summer's day was not enhanced by the exhaust in the wake of the V2 however, there was a slight incline and the train appears well loaded. *R.H.Leslie.*

With steam to spare A4 No.60005 SIR CHARLES NEWTON accelerates south past the photographer as it leaves Black Carr junction in its wake on 23rd April 1962. *A.R.Thompson.*

Having travelled 153 miles from King's Cross, we have now reached the multi junction at Black Carr, just over two miles south of Doncaster station. The first noticeable feature of this place is the huge skew girder bridge which carried the Dearne Valley Railway over the ECML. Next is the number of signals about the place which were accompanied by three signal boxes. Finally the amount of traffic and number of routes reveals why so many signals were required. The date is 14th October 1961 and another Gresley A4 No.60026 MILES BEEVOR, running freely with a London bound express, is our first encounter at the juction. *A.R.Thompson.*

23

Moving a few hundred yards further north, beyond the skew bridge, we come across, Doncaster 9F No.92190 which was 'pegged' for the Gainsborough line at it closes on the junction at Black Carr with a Doncaster Decoy-March freight in 1961. *P.J.Robinson.*

Doncaster based V2 No.60872 KING'S OWN YORKSHIRE LIGHT INFANTRY joins the Down fast on the ECML from the Joint line at Black Carr junction with an express of unknown origin but possibly a Colchester-York and Newcastle working in 1960. From the GE's termini at Liverpool Street the journey over the Joint line to this location amounted to some 180 miles! However, the route became a very important freight route and took a lot of pressure off the ECML. All along its length, the Joint line was traversed by other routes belonging to the Great Central and the Great Northern. The Great Eastern remained steadfastly fixed to the Joint all the way to Whitemoor yard and March where their territory began in earnest. This particular passenger train may well have been a diverted ECML express but there were also a number of important passenger workings over the GN&GE Joint too. In the right background is the flyover featured earlier, which carried the DVR over the ECML. *P.J.Robinson. (right)* Straight to the point; a Dearne Valley Railway public notice located between two routes. *F.W.Hampson.*

DEARNE VALLEY RAILWAY
PUBLIC NOTICE
ALL PERSONS ARE HEREBY WARNED NOT TO TRESPASS ON THIS LINE.
EVERY PERSON SO TRESPASSING AFTER THIS NOTICE WILL BE PROSECUTED AND WILL BE LIABLE TO A PENALTY NOT EXCEEDING FORTY SHILLINGS
BY ORDER.

On a bright 23rd April 1962, A4 No.60007 SIR NIGEL GRESLEY accelerates through the junction with an Up express. In the background is the bridge carrying the Doncaster avoiding lines which linked Kirk Sandall junction with numerous south Yorkshire collieries and the former GC Worksop-Sheffield main line. To the right are the lines to Gainsborough and the Great Northern-Great Eastern Joint line. *A.R.Thompson.*

On 14th October 1961, K3 No.61918 runs off the Joint line onto the Down slow of the ECML opposite Black Carr Junction signal box with a Down freight. Though the running lines are nowadays reduced in number, this junction is still of great importance. The last semaphore signal at this place was not taken down until September 1978 and, it was apparently the last such signal on the ECML! *A.R.Thompson.*

27

A little earlier on that October Saturday in 1961, Gresley O2 No.63983 was photographed from virtually the same spot. It too was coming off the Joint line with a long mixed freight in tow from Whitemoor marshalling yard to Doncaster Decoy yard. It is now late afternoon and the train probably left March earlier in the morning, covering the ninety-odd miles comfortably within the enginemen's shift. The goods traffic still running on British Railways at that time was generating revenue and such was the demand on line occupation that freights were being worked on Saturday afternoons when most of the nation had 'knocked-off' for the weekend. In the right background, at a point just above the middle of the visible train, can be seen another girder bridge which carried the Up line from the DVR over the Up and Down Joint lines. That particular Up line met the Up Joint line at Bessacarr junction. And so we follow the 2-8-0 on to Doncaster. *F.W.Hampson.*

Having reached the engine shed at Doncaster Carr, we can stroll around the place to look at some of the inhabitants on this Saturday afternoon, 13th October 1962. In the north yard an unidentified WD is shunting three post-Grouping J50s to create some space for the weekend lodgers which could swell the population of the depot to a hundred or so locomotives by Sunday morning. The three 0-6-0Ts from nearest are Nos.68971, 68961 and 68976; all of them have a nice coating of grime which will remain with them until scrapped but they had something else in common – they were all withdrawn although appearances would indicate otherwise. No.68971 had become part of the Departmental fleet (16th September 1962) to shunt the locomotive works at Doncaster as Dept'l. No.15. In reality, the J50 did not take up that number for another year at least; it was finally condemned at the end of May 1965. No.68976 followed the same course, and on the same dates and became Dept'l. No.16. No.68961 which was also part of the same batch of J50s withdrawn for Departmental use on 16th September 1962 (68917 [No.12] and 68928 [No.13] were the others) was the longest lived of the group and was not condemned until 19th September 1965; this engine retained its smokebox numberplate whilst in works employment and, perhaps more bizarre, it somehow managed to keep a 34B Hornsey shedplate attached even though it had transferred from that shed in July 1961 to New England, then to Doncaster 36A in June 1962. Nothing was straightforward. They were interesting times. *A.Ives.*

On the previous Sunday, 7th October 1962, the south end of the shed yard hosted three A4s amongst the usual B1s. From left to right this line-up consists Nos.60017 SILVER FOX (King's Cross), 61250 A.HAROLD BIBBY (New England), 60032 GANNET (King's Cross), 61158 (Doncaster), and 60029 WOODCOCK (King's Cross). None of the Pacifics had attended works and had worked into Doncaster on various trains. *A.R.Thompson.*

Close-up of A4 WOODCOCK on that same Sunday in October 1962! Two 9F 2-10-0s are visible: No.92168 and 92201; five and four years old respectively! *I.W.Coulson.*

Remaining in the south yard at Doncaster shed we present another King's Cross A4 in 1962: No.60010 DOMINION OF CANADA. The Pacific is brewing-up prior to working home. In mid-June 1963, along with the other surviving A4s at 34A, this engine was transferred to New England for a life of uncertainty. However, circumstances dictated that a certain class of diesel locomotive based in Scotland would become something of a liability for British Railways and because no suitable alternative diesel power was available to work the express trains between Aberdeen and Glasgow, certain redundant A4s would be transferred to Ferryhill shed where most of the conscripted engines got at least a couple of years further employment prior to scrapping. This example was different because it was presented to Canada and shipped over there in April 1967. *A.R.Thompson.*

A nice trio of front ends on 7th October 1962. Note the lamps are all in different positions – right, left, and centre! *A.R. Thompson.*

33

During the period when the engine shed was being re-roofed in the late 1950s, enthusiasts were neither deterred nor prohibited from walking around the depot. On 14th June 1958 A3 No.60079 BAYARDO presents a sight for sore eyes as it languishes on the north yard after a visit to works for a General overhaul. Since nationalisation the Carlisle Canal Pacific was otherwise something of a stranger in these parts and only ventured south of the border for reasons such as works attention. It was on one such visit in September 1961 which saw the A3 condemned and later cut up at 'The Plant' works. Note the Stanier tender just muscling into the photograph. *C.J.B.Sanderson.*

A trio of Pacifics – Peppercorn A2 No.60533 HAPPY KNIGHT and Thompson A2/3 No.60523 SUN CASTLE, along with an unidentified Peppercorn A1 – grace the south yard at Doncaster shed on Saturday evening, 5th August 1961; both A2s were residents. The Peppercorn A2 was something of a nomad in so far as having had fourteen shed transfers since it was put into traffic thirteen years earlier; admittedly most had been shared between Grantham and especially New England, with perhaps the most bizarre amongst them being a week spent at Annesley from 2nd to 9th July 1950; a final transfer to New England in September 1962 would be its last. Co-incidentally it was condemned at New England on 15th June 1963, just as the former King's Cross A4s started to arrive at 34E. Doncaster built No.60533 entered the works during the first week of September for scrapping. No.60523 likewise transferred from Doncaster to New England in September 1962 and it too was condemned at 34E just as the 'Top Shed' Pacifics arrived! Another product of Doncaster, No.60523 was taken into works for cutting up just a week prior to No.60533. *C.Campbell.*

35

On Sunday 17th July 1955, Thompson A2/2 No.60504 MONS MEG forms the centrepiece of what had been the previous Friday's cavalcade from the 'Plant' to Carr shed. No.60504 had been in the shops for six weeks receiving a General overhaul where the boiler was removed, repaired and then put back; not the usual procedure at Doncaster or most other works which usually fitted a refurbished boiler once the old one was lifted out of the frames. Compared with the Gresley Pacifics, the Thompson A2s tended to be fitted with fewer boilers and this engine had only two throughout its time from rebuilding from P2 class in 1944 to withdrawal in January 1961. After this time in shops, the New England A2 had to revisit the works no less than five times during the next six months to rectify a problem which had shown up during post-overhaul running-in. Also in the line-up is a new BR Standard Class 4 bound for the Southern Region, probably No.76061, which would give a lot less trouble to the fitters. *I.S.Carr.*

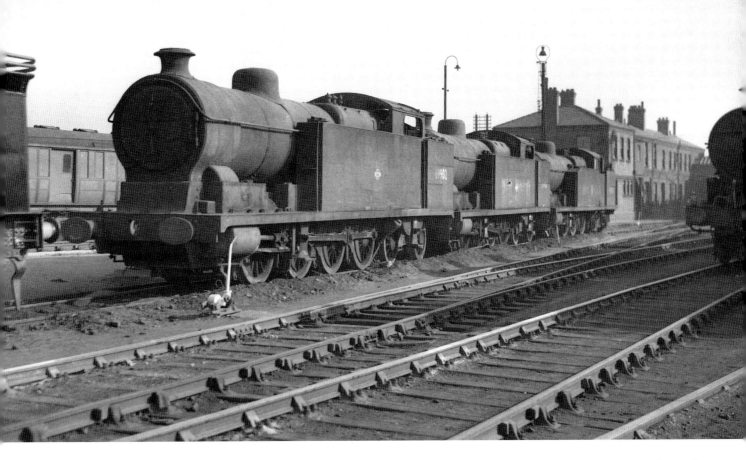

Doncaster shed played host to many different locomotive types which were either visiting after working into the area, or attending main works for attention of one sort or another. On Sunday 16th October 1955, this trio of massive S1 0-8-4 tank engines – Nos.69902, 69900, and 69904 – was doing neither of those things; they were residents of 36A and had been for nearly two years. Admittedly, they did very little, if any, work whilst at Doncaster and in this position in the north yard they remained huddled together for many months during 1955. Nos.69900 and 69904 were both condemned on 6th January 1956; 69902 followed on 13th January. On 18th February 1956 Nos.69900 and 69902 were sent to Gorton for cutting up but that event did not take place at the Manchester works and they were both packed off to Darlington for scrapping. No.69904, at the far end of the bunch in view here, was sent directly to Darlington after the other two had been refused attention at Gorton. Perhaps, later in the series, as we journey ever further north, we might catch up with one or more of this trio in residence at Darlington scrapyard. *F.W.Hampson.*

Class leader No.70000 BRITANNIA looks resplendent on the shed yard on 26th September 1959 after having received a heavy overhaul whereby its third boiler since new had been fitted. AWS was also fitted at this shopping and the receiver can be seen just beneath the bufferbeam. Allocated to Stratford since being put into traffic in January 1951, No.70000 transferred to Norwich in February 1959. This was the period just before the 'Brits' lost their standing as the 'top dogs' on the GE main line to the English Electric Type 4 diesels. By the summer of 1961 the GE line had relegated their 'Brits' to working secondary and freight services, concentrating them at March shed. In 1963, after a period in store, the ER engines were all transferred to the LMR where further use could be made of them prior to withdrawal. Our subject here was of course eventually preserved, a fitting end to an engine which heralded the proper standardisation of BR steam locomotion. Whilst this Pacific is made ready to make its way back to Norfolk, we must move onwards and northwards. *C.J.B.Sanderson.*

En route from Carr locomotive shed to Doncaster's main line station (named Central from 1923-1951) you passed firstly beneath Balby Bridge tunnel and then a little further on beneath St James's bridge also. From the north parapet of the latter you got an excellent view of the main line to the north, and the passenger station. In the space between the two bridges, on the left, Down side, two junctions and a set of carriage sidings were located. The first, known as Bridge junction swung westwards off the main line and joined the lines from the next junction – South Yorkshire junction – which brought the lines from the Rotherham and Sheffield direction onto the ECML just to the south of Doncaster station. Going onto St James's bridge as a pedestrian, and walking to its western end, you could look over the south parapet and glancing in the Rotherham direction you would have been greeted with this view – well you were on 23rd October 1960, and for some time afterwards I should imagine. This is a private scrapyard created on the former cattle dock of St James's Bridge station goods depot. St James's Bridge passenger station – long closed by this time – was just out of frame to the left but its adjacent goods depot, actually called Cherrytree goods, complete with goods shed, stands beyond the carnage atop the cattle dock. Some sixteen Churchill main battle tanks, apparently of a later Mark, are crammed into the yard and are in various stages of dismantling. How long the vehicles had been resident is unknown as is the method used to transport them here, and from where. Exact details of the tanks are unknown to this compiler so perhaps one of our readers might be able to enlighten us. Known facts about the Churchill tank are as follows: 7,368 were produced between 1941 and 1945; no less than thirteen different marks, not including specialist vehicles were built mainly by Vauxhall Motors but BRC&WC produced some too; they were in service with the British Army from 1941 to 1952 and served in all the major theatres of war including the Korean conflict; weighing in at between 38 and 40 tons, they had a top speed of just 15 m.p.h. but they were heavily armoured with thickness ranging from 16mm to 152 mm; main armament ranged from an initial 2 pounder gun to a 75 mm gun in later models; the Churchill was ultimately replaced by the Centurion tank. Other clues as to origin are a couple of visible registrations: 10ZV25; 12ZV07; 18ZV24. Later, we move on to another more topical scrapyard. *N.W.Skinner.*

The usual view captured by photographers from St James's bridge. Looking north towards the station in the mid-1950s we see B16 No.61422 heading south with two new but unidentified Darlington-built 0-6-0DE shunters. In line with the end of this special working, note Doncaster's main-line pilot on its daily vigil. *R.F.Payne.*

The New Erecting shop at Doncaster was responsible for some of the more iconic LNER designs such as the Gresley A4s but when British Railways came into being the shop was entrusted to produce many of the less glamorous BR Standard steam locomotive types. Amongst them were forty-two Class 5 4-6-0s (73100-73124 and 73155-73171) between 1955 and 1957. The years between 1952 and 1957 saw seventy Class 4 2-6-0 tender engines (76020-76074 and 76100 to 76114) built whilst in 1954 ten Class 4 tank engines (80106-80115) were turned-out for the Scottish Region. Before the first examples of that lot were even started in late 1952, this shop was busy building fifty of the Ivatt LMS designed Class 4F 2-6-0 tender engines (43050-43069, 43107-43111, 43137-43161) from 1950 to 1952. The last steam locomotive built at Doncaster was one of the BR Std. Cl.4s, No.76114, which was put into traffic during October 1957. After the end of steam work, electric traction became the 'bread and butter' for this shop and in 1958 the first of a batch of twenty-four 2,552 horsepower, 750V d.c. Bo-Bo electric locomotives (E5000-E5023) for the Southern Region were built. Of course these were not the first electrics Doncaster had built because the works was responsible for building the iconic Manchester-Sheffield-Wath Bo-Bo 6701 (26000) in 1940 as the prototype for a class originally to number seventy. By 1960 Doncaster started to build the 3,300 h.p. 25 kV a.c. locomotives for the WCML and here on Sunday 23rd October 1960 is the first of that batch, E3056, complete with its overall blue livery inside the erecting shop. On the left another body is being put together whilst completed bogies fill the right hand road. Strangely, Doncaster was not involved with building any diesel locomotives, other than the 0-6-0DM Drewry shunters, until the introduction of the Class 56 Co-Cos in 1977. Note the maintenance men working on the overhead crane tracks! *N.W.Skinner.*

One of the New Erecting shop's earlier products outside the Weigh shed in the works yard on Sunday 18th August 1957. With just five more of these BR Std. Cl.4s to be completed, Doncaster's long tradition of turning out more than two thousand steam locomotives would soon be over. No.76109 cost, according to the Engine Record Card, £20,648 to build, including the tender. The 2-6-0 was however destined for a rather short life on the Scottish Region working initially from Thornton Junction shed and then from Dunfermline where it was condemned in September 1966. Note the newly applied but wrong facing BR crest. This locomotive would have been one of the earliest recipients of that new crest. *D.Fairley.*

One of Doncaster's works shunters from the early 1950s or so it would seem. Sentinel Dept'l. No.7 was formerly No.68166 in Capital Stock but it gave up that status in March 1953 when it began official employment in Departmental Stock at Boston's Hall Hills Sleeper Depot. The little four-wheeled engine had actually been employed at that establishment since April 1940 but had slipped through the net in 1948 and was numbered 68166. This undated view, with a Pacific boiler behind (No.29873 and E520 are marked on the lower flank. The boiler was fitted to A2/3 No.60520 from 17th January 1959 [ex A1 No.60114] to 29th March 1961), is in the boiler park but the presence of the Sentinel helps date the illustration to a period in the spring or summer of 1961. The A2 boiler had, it appears just been removed from 60520 whereas the Sentinel had arrived at Doncaster for a General overhaul on 20th March 1961 but was now awaiting a slot in the Crimpsall shop. Leaving Doncaster for the last time on 21st July 1961, No.7 was destined for a new home at Lowestoft Civil Engineers Depot where it worked until May 1964. So, we can confidently date this image between April and June 1961. A similar but dated photograph captured by another photographer from a reverse angle dates this scene as 17th May 1961. Now, you ask 'Why the E prefix on the boiler at such a late date?' A.R.Thompson.

Alongside Doncaster's Crimpsall shops on Sunday 23rd October 1960 was one of the works boiler trolleys fashioned from a set of C1 Atlantic locomotive frames. The origin of this one is unknown but it was numbered 5 in that unique fleet and beneath the number was a date given as 8-12-56 with a prefix LEP. The load appears to be a Pacific boiler, minus tubes! *N.W.Skinner.*

When C1 Atlantic No.62822 was condemned on 27th November 1950 (the last of its kind), it had been parted from its normal Class B tender (No.T5078) two days beforehand but was then coupled to another Class B (T5054) which was fitted with a water scoop, until 1st December 1950, when it then lost that one and was coupled to the Class A tender in the illustration (T1306). To assist moving the engines about the works, it was sometimes necessary to couple them up with a completely 'foreign' tender once their own tender had been taken away hence the unusual couplings featured. The Class A tender was ex Class D3 4-4-0 No.2181 which had been condemned in November 1950 and had parted with its tender on the 20th of that month. To complicate matters, this illustration is undated but we can assume it was captured on film during that final month of 1950 if not the first weeks of 1951. Tender 1306 was sold to private industry in January 1951; this was a regular occurrence at Doncaster because of its proximity to two steel producing areas where tenders were used as either water carriers or, when cut down to frames only, for carrying billets. Back to our C1, it might be worth relating to its tender coupling record (all Class B) which can be traced back to 19th January 1928 when it was coupled to T5035 until 11th June 1932. From 23rd July 1932 to 15th May 1943 it was mated with T5193. T5130 was the next coupling from 12th June 1943 to 5th October 1945 (gaps in dates indicate period when the engine was in shops). To take it into BR ownership the C1 was coupled to T5152 from 5th October 1945 to 11th February 1949. T5078 came onto the scene then to be followed by T5054. That final Class B tender had been borrowed from K2 No.61736 so that the C1 could take part in the haulage of a special non-stop train from King's Cross to Doncaster on Sunday 26th November 1950. T5054 was returned to No.61736 on 1st December 1950. No.61736 had been the custodian of T5078 during that last week of November. Coupled to O2 No.63935 from 31st January 1951 to 26th November 1961, T5078 went on to survive until it was cut up at Doncaster on 25th November 1961. No.62822 itself was finally cut up at Doncaster in May 1951, sans tender of any kind. This C1 was notable as being the last of her kind to work in normal traffic. The smokebox numberplate has been removed (another notable as being the only C1 to carry one and that same plate is now in the safe keeping of Doncaster Grammar school), but the 35B Grantham shedplate remains in situ. *K.H.Cockerill.* 45

A pair of contrasting Doncaster Pacifics for your delectation: *(above)* Edward Thompson's tribute to himself is manifested in A2/3 No.500, seen on the shed yard at Doncaster in October 1946. *C.J.B.Sanderson. (below)* Peppercorn A1 No.60126 (it wasn't named until August 1950) stands in the works yard at Doncaster on Sunday 24th April 1949 looking every bit the totally proportioned machine incorporating elegance and power. Both of these illustrations depict events which are actually outside of our date parameters for the series but I'm sure most, if not all, of you will forgive us for this little indulgence. Furthermore, the two pictures together were to form a link between the shed and the works but that didn't quite work out to be the case. *K.H.Cockerill.*

Back to the remit, we have this unusual view of a virtually legless Britannia Pacific No.70036 BOADICEA which is also nearly married up to an A3 GN tender. The date is 13th October 1962 – note the new building work progressing – and the Immingham based 'Brit' appears to have been taken out of the shops and 'parked-up' whilst work on its coupled wheels proceeds elsewhere, seemingly slowly. By this time Doncaster had apparently given up its responsibility to overhaul and repair the Eastern Region 'Brits' to the works at Crewe from June 1962 so the presence of No.70036 would indicate an urgent, perhaps non-classified repair. *A.Ives.*

How about this engine-tender marriage? Immingham B1 No.61144 quite suits the A3 tender – perhaps moreso if the green was changed to black livery. The date is circa May 1955 and the 4-6-0 has just completed a General overhaul (12th April to 17th May) ready to go back into traffic. The identification of the tender is unknown. *J.W.Armstrong.*

Quite a rare visitor to this section of the ECML was Aberdeen Ferryhill's Peppercorn A2 No.60528 TUDOR MINSTREL. **Tenderless in the works yard on Sunday 7th May 1961, the Pacific had been in shops since 20th March receiving a Casual Light repair which appears to have involved work at the front end – those bogie wheels look suspiciously new. During the following morning the 61B engine was coupled to its tender and hauled off to the shed ready to go back into traffic and return home. It would come back to Doncaster one final time during the summer of 1962 when it received a General overhaul, reconditioned boiler, and a fresh coat of paint; all of which stood it in good stead for another four years work before withdrawal. Doncaster based O2 No.63985, standing immediately behind, has just had its final works overhaul, a General, and would join the A2 in the cavalcade back to Carr engine shed on the morrow'.** *N.W.Skinner.*

A3 No.60061 PRETTY POLLY had just arrived at Doncaster for a General overhaul when it was photographed on the works yard on Saturday morning 6th January 1962. The King's Cross based Pacific wears the small side vanes on the smokebox which were fairly recent fittings to help eliminate drifting smoke and steam obscuring vision from the cab. This engine was one of four A3s – Nos.60048, 60055 and 60112 being the others – chosen in 1958 to be fitted with double blastpipe and chimney. However, the softer blast of the double blastpipe did not lift the exhaust high enough from the chimney resulting in drifting smoke being blown along the boiler. The side vanes were supposed to 'fix' the problem but too little air to create an upward draught was generated by the vanes! The same problem and half-hearted solution had been encountered twenty-odd years previously when HUMORIST was fitted with Kylchap double blastpipe and chimney but nobody in 1958 appears to have taken any notice of history. Eventually of course the answer lay in fitting the big trough style smoke deflectors and fifty-five of the class were so fitted. PRETTY POLLY got them during this overhaul. Note the water scoop fitments on the ground. *Ian Falcus.*

Some years earlier in April 1955, one of the GC main line A3s had just completed a 'General' when it was photographed near to the paint shop prior to leaving works. No.60052 PRINCE PALATINE had been allocated to Leicester Central shed in May 1949 and except for a five month stint at Neasden in late 1954, it remained at 38C until transferred back to ECML working at the end of August 1955. This Pacific turned out to be one of the great survivors of the class inasmuch that it was operational until January 1966. One of the main reasons for its longer life span, compared with other A3s, was its transfer to Scottish Region and St Margarets shed in particular during August 1963. *K.H.Cockerill.*

Although Gorton was responsible for the overhauls and the general well being of the O4 and Thompson O1 rebuilds, Doncaster started to take in the March-based O1s long before the former GC workshops closed. On Saturday 19th May 1962 Thompson O1 No.63746 had just completed a 'General' and would be signed-off on Tuesday 22nd. However, three weeks later the 2-8-0 was back in shops for a Non-Classified repair which usually entailed rectification of a problem found after the General overhaul had been finished. Once Gorton works had closed in 1963, all the 2-8-0 repairs normally undertaken there were transferred to Doncaster, including the WD 2-8-0 overhauls. Note the O1 classification applied to the bufferbeam, something Gorton didn't always carry out. In the right background can be seen A3 No.60061 complete with its German smoke deflectors. The Pacific had just come into works for a Casual Light repair and was just about to be towed back to Carr shed. *H.Forster.*

You could be forgiven for thinking that this image illustrates part of the works scrapyard on 7th May 1961 but that is not in fact the case. However, K1/1 No.61997 MACCAILIN MOR had arrived in works two weeks earlier on 24th April from Fort William shed and was being assessed for repair. In the event it failed and was condemned five weeks later on 12th June. Behind is D2402, one of the ten Andrew Barclay diesel-mechanical shunters supplied to the Eastern Region in 1956 and which had just been renumbered from its original 11179. The little 0-6-0DM survived its works visit and continued working until withdrawn in September 1967 when British Railways was condemning all of the non-standard diesel types. Whatever was ailing the 2-6-0, it took long enough to assess before a decision was finally made. Perhaps its singular existence as the only K1/1 played a part because even then, British Railways were scrapping non-standard types of steam locomotive too. *N.W.Skinner.*

Another definite non-standard steam locomotive living a precarious existence by the late 1950s was W1 No.60700. This view of 23rd May 1959 shows off the unusually large cab of the streamliner to best effect; it must have been a heck of a distance for the fireman to shovel the coal from the tender to the firebox and would no doubt require a great degree of accuracy too. The illustration also shows the rear pony wheels and their relationship with each other and the rest of the locomotive. The 4-6-4, or was it really a 4-6-2-2, had entered works two weeks beforehand and was now just one week away from being condemned. It was cut up shortly afterwards. *Alan Brooks.*

Having led you here by a roundabout route, we arrive at the scrapyard. Doncaster's scrap men had always had a healthy appetite for condemned locomotives and even when other workshops temporarily ceased the cutting up of locomotives at various periods, Doncaster was always ready to receive their discarded hulks. Such was the case with both Gorton and Stratford who, even in the 1930s, had sent most of their withdrawn locomotives to Doncaster. In late March 1952 this was the scene in the scrapyard as this ex-GNR 2-8-0, O3 class No.63476, was being dismantled. Condemned on 17th of that month, the 2-8-0 had last served at Retford but was by now getting rather 'long in the tooth' at nearly forty years old. Its final major overhaul had taken place in August 1950 when it was given boiler No.21000. That particular boiler was, it will be noted, quite intact whereas much of the locomotive had been cut. The reason why the boiler was still in one piece was because it was sound enough for re-use and went on to serve no less than three Class O2 engines before finally being condemned in July 1961, when attached to O2 No.63957. On the left is another casualty of March 1952 – D1 No.65008 which had the instructions – conn & coup rods wtd – chalked on the cab side sheet. *K.H.Cockerill.*

During late 1959 and early 1960, the scrapyard at Doncaster underwent a massive improvement whereby a new large, 30-ton capacity overhead crane was installed by the Glasgow firm of Carruthers. The idea was to enable Doncaster to deal with more than the usual throughput as diesel locomotives started to accelerate the redundancy of steam motive power. One of the first noticeable changes was the acceptance by Doncaster of other regions condemned locomotives, especially those from Derby where a backlog had been building throughout 1959. This is Doncaster scrap yard on Sunday 8th May 1960 with ex-Somerset & Dorset 2-8-0 No.53802 awaiting attention and surrounded by other former Midland products. The new overhead crane will oversee the approaching carnage. *N.W.Skinner.*

Anyone approaching the works from the River Don's new cut or canal, and not being aware of the situation concerning Doncaster and the LMR cast-offs might well think he was at Derby during 1960. This was part of the yard on Sunday 23rd October 1960 with LMS-built 2P No.40581 in the latter stages of its demise. Note the 1928 Derby works plate is still in situ on the leading splasher. I wonder what happened to that? *N.W.Skinner.*

And so it went on into 1963. The one-off 'exotics' such as the S&D 2-8-0 were one thing but when most of the condemned LT&SR line 4P 2-6-4Ts came to be dealt with at Doncaster we knew a phenomenon was taking place. However, the taking in of the Derby overspill was a different matter than the cutting up of the 2-6-4Ts because those very same locomotives from the London Tilbury line were now, and had been for some time, the responsibility of the Eastern Region which meant that Doncaster had to deal with them; that would have been the argument according to Derby anyway as each region tried to get rid of its unwanted scrap in any way possible. On Sunday 7th April 1963, 4P No.42530 of the aforementioned tank engines was resident along with A3 No.60111 ENTERPRISE. The latter had entered the yard on the previous Wednesday complete with smokebox numberplate and both nameplates but the shed plate had been removed. Note that the 2-6-4T carried nothing 'valuable' by this time, however, note also that some wag has placed a piece of fire grating on the centre lamp iron in the style of the destination boards once carried by these 3-cylinder locomotives. *N.W.Skinner.*

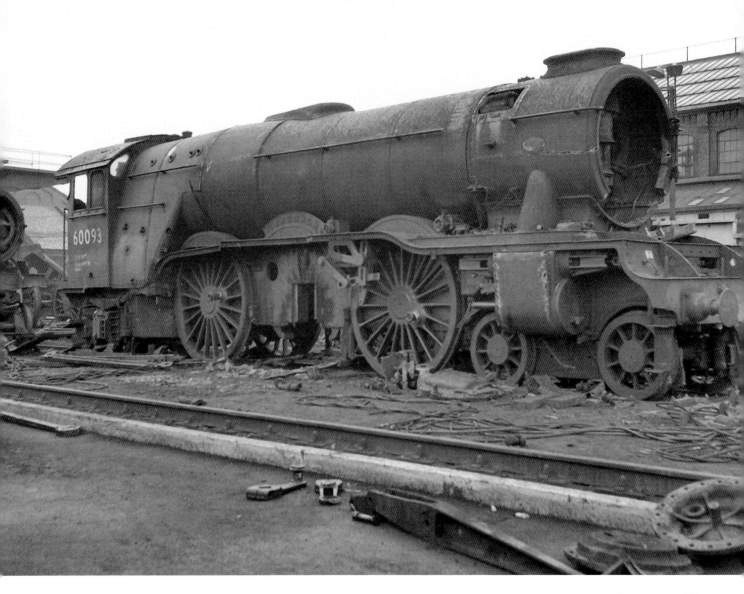

During the interim period Doncaster had managed to cut up a lot of former LNER locomotives including numerous Pacifics. In May 1962 for instance ex-Carlisle Canal A3 No.60093 CORONACH was being dealt with after its 24th April condemnation. Looking at the state of the livery, especially the boiler top, it appears that No.60093 had not worked for some time prior to being withdrawn but it had attended Doncaster over the Christmas period of 1961 for a Casual Light repair so the time out of service could only have been a matter of weeks. One thing for certain is that CORONACH was never going to work again. Note that although the worksplate has been removed, probably during the process of flame cutting the smokebox, the nameplate is still fixed to the splasher. *I.W.Coulson.*

Returning to the station we see one of the shed-to-works cavalcades en route with WD No.90001 hauling J50 No.68975 and A3 No.60096 PAPYRUS to the 'Plant' on 29th July 1961. The Haymarket Pacific was going in for a General, its last, whilst the King's Cross based 0-6-0T was just hours away from being condemned. The Doncaster based 'Austerity' was just having an easy day on the works shuttle. Within an hour or so No.90001 would return to the shed with a batch of newly refurbished and repaired locomotives, some gleaming with new coats of glossy paint, others perhaps not – the daily grind of Doncaster locomotive works. *H.Forster.*

Spotted in the Down side bay at the north end of the station on 16th July 1961 was this former Great Northern Railway carriage with BR fleet number E 468 E, and extra marking 'LN3 'at the end. It appears to be a Full Brake with an off-set corridor connection; the buffer beneath the connection has been trimmed at the top to allow the clear passage of the connection. Built in 1920, the vehicle's original number was probably No.954. It was rebuilt as a postal storage van, hence the off-set gangway connection, which was a later addition, making it impossible for the public to access the van. Advice on distributing a 10-ton load is painted onto the lower body beneath the number. Note that the roof is much higher than that on the adjacent GUV and forms an almost perfect radius. The carriage works where this vehicle was probably built decades beforehand forms the background of the illustration. *N.W.Skinner.*

On an unrecorded date some years earlier when the old canopies still stood, a Darlington based A5 and an unidentified sister try out the newly laid trackwork at the south end of the Up main platform. Why these two Pacific tanks from the North Eastern Region should be so far south is uncertain but a trip to Gorton works cannot be ruled out because a number of the Hawthorn Leslie built engines of this class, which normally attended only Darlington or Gateshead works for repairs and overhauls, went to the Manchester shops for a heavy overhauls during the second half of 1954. No.69830 was not however one of them so may well have been delivering a sister engine; its allocation record at 51A coincides nicely with the period in question (19th September 1954 to 15th September 1957). For the record, the following were at Gorton for heavy overhauls during 1954: Nos.69831 – 14th August to 2nd October; 69832 – 2nd October to 20th November; 69834 – 10th July to 4th September; 69837 – 18th September to 23rd October; 69838 – 18th September to 30th October; 69840 – 5th June to 10th July; 69841 – 8th to 15th May (Casual Light so may well have taken itself?); 69843 – 18th September to 30th October. Note that some of the 'out' dates coincide with some of the 'in' dates which would then enable the towing engine to work both ways under a 'revenue' working rather than returning home light engine. However, without the exact date of this image we cannot be totally sure about any of the above so it is left to you the reader to decide. *K.H.Cockerill.*

Waiting for the next chime whistle, spotters' appear only half interested in the dirty black engine from York as B16 No.61464 waits for the 'right away' with an afternoon working back home from the newly refurbished Down platform in the summer of 1959. From personal memories, Doncaster station was a trainspotters haven as long as you behaved and most, if not all, did so. *I.S.Carr.*

63

Even in 1949 the spotters' appeared to have free reign at Doncaster station. The date is 19th March, a Saturday so no questions asked, as three youngsters admire one of Mr Thompson's B1s – yet to be renumbered 1082 – starting out from the Up platform with a train of pure LNER stock bound for Cleethorpes via Gainsborough. By now Doncaster station's main building, the roof of which is visible above the leading carriage, is fully occupied after World War Two retarded its completion in 1941. The centre section of the footbridge to the 'Plant' works was replaced by a more substantial structure in 1953 (*see* later) but the one-time passenger footbridge which ran parallel was taken down pre-war. The original platform awnings covering each of the platform roads of 4 and 5 are still in situ. Replacement for those would take a lot longer to materialise but when it was carried out it opened up the area of the four through lines between platforms 4 and 5. The electric lamp posts gracing platform 4 were also fairly new having been part of the station rebuilding scheme started in 1937 but they too would disappear by 1960 as BR's own version of modernisation started to unfold. *K.H.Cockerill.*

Gresley A3 No.60111 ENTERPRISE – before it got those German type smoke deflectors – runs through the station with a heavy Down express during the evening of Saturday 5th August 1961. One of the oldest Gresley Pacifics, and Doncaster built too (to traffic 17th August 1923 as LNER 1480), this was also one of the earliest rebuilds from A1 to A3 class (9th May to 15th July 1927). By now it was a Grantham engine; the same depot from where it started its operational career in 1923 and from where it ended thirty-nine years later. In the left background is the church which gave its name to the bridge in the distance and the station just around the corner on the Rotherham line. *H.Forster.*

Further locomotive variety one year later – with ever increasing numbers of diesel locomotives, including the 'Deltics', arriving on the ECML to work the passenger expresses by the summer of 1962, steam motive power was starting to become the exception rather than the norm. On Saturday 25th August 1962 one of Doncaster's A2/3s, No.60520 OWEN TUDOR, runs through its home town with a Down express whilst working one of those diagrams which kept it away from 36A for a couple of days. It transferred to New England at the end of the '62 summer timetable. Note the lack of trainspotters on this date. *H.Forster.*

(above) A3 No.60084 TRIGO stands at platform 4 with a King's Cross bound express from Newcastle as a wheeltapper gets to work on the first bogie of the afternoon train on 25th August 1962. At this time No.60084 was a Neville Hill engine so was not too common around these parts especially since the previous January when it attended the 'Plant' works for the last time. Transferring to Gateshead in December 1963, the A3 continued working for another year before withdrawal. It was sold to a scrap yard in North Blyth in January 1965. Diesel multiple units have now taken over on the services to Cleethorpes and Lincoln, one of their ilk, E50001 is sitting in bay platform 3. *H.Forster. (below)* On 29th July 1961, A4 No.60028 WALTER K.WHIGHAM runs along the Up main with what appears to be the Saturday service of *THE ELIZABETHAN*. The deserted footbridge leading to the works would have made a superb vantage point for photographers but alas the bridge was out of bounds to all except 'Plant' personnel. Note the new section spanning the through main lines and adjacent platforms. *Ian Falcus.*

With just nine vehicles in tow, MALLARD is making light work of this Up express on 23rd May 1959. Even then, d.m.us. were well entrenched on certain 'local' services. The Cravens unit at platform 4 is a return service to Hull with E50359 trailing. *I.S.Carr.*

Sunday, 12th May 1963 and Doncaster's young platform-enders' were probably dumbfounded by the appearance of a totally foreign but nevertheless very welcome addition to their lists. Southern Region 'West Country' No.34094 MORTEHOE, of Nine Elms shed, has arrived at platform 5 from the south with a Warwickshire Railway Society special (1X36). The route taken and the reason for its visit to Doncaster are unknown but certainly caused a stir not seen perhaps since the 1948 Locomotive Exchanges. Of course as the years prior to the end of steam unfolded, more and more exotic locomotives began to be used for society railtours which took them to all sorts of places as a sort of one-upmanship appeared to emerge. However, the mindset then was that once steam had finished on British Railways, the running of such locomotives would be impossible because they would not exist (FLYING SCOTSMAN'S preservation was still in its infancy and nobody had ever purchased such big engines before, never mind run them) and even if they did in small numbers, BR would not allow them onto the main line. So, in those transitional days it was use what you could get away with whilst you could; the good times are not going to last much longer! How little we knew of what the future was going to bring. This SR Pacific was fairly unique in a strange sort of way because it was one of the few of her kind which entered Woodham's yard at Barry and never came out. Withdrawn in August 1964, it was taken into the south Wales yard and cut up with indecent haste by the end of the following November! *H.Forster.*

Time to leave Doncaster now and head north to our next destination – Selby! During the afternoon of Saturday 19th March 1949, a three-month old Peppercorn A1 No.60139 (SEA EAGLE from May 1950) runs through the station with the Down *QUEEN OF SCOTS* Pullman which would have been ideal transport but that train would deviate left at Marshgate junction, towards Leeds, soon after leaving Doncaster station behind. We however are proceeding due north. The *QofS* will rejoin the ECML some distance to the north of here at Northallerton after a somewhat tortuous route via a reversal at Leeds (Central), then on through Harrogate, Wetherby and back onto the main line; a nice journey in the summer, with a late night arrival in Glasgow (Queens Street) but during the winter, in the dark, it could be long and tedious with reliance on table service and endless refreshments. This final view of Doncaster, looking south, reveals St James bridge in the distance whilst nearer is the fairly new, then, South signal box (fully commissioned on Sunday 9th January 1949) and its associated directional colour light signals. Spotters' inhabit both Up and Down platforms, the platform luggage trolleys becoming temporary settees, sofas or even beds! Whereas Crewe had its platform enders' shouting 'Semi!' whenever a 'Duchess' appeared, Doncaster's lot hollered 'Streak' just to get the shivers running down your spine before the mighty beasts sounded their chime whistles which certainly did bring on a sensation worth waiting for. I hope Doncaster has proved to be as interesting for you as it has for me. In the heady days of the 50s' and 60s' it certainly was the place to be if you wanted diversification of ER steam, and diesel! *K.H.Cockerill.*

On the approach to Selby station we meet G5 No.67250 working a local service past Selby South signal box and its adjacent, impressive, gantry. The Up platform of the station is just visible beneath the span of Park Street bridge. The track nearest is the Down main from Leeds which joined the ECML at this spot. *J.W.Armstrong.*

(above) We have arrived at Selby station just as a York-Doncaster 'local' service has stopped with Peppercorn A1 No.60153 FLAMBOYANT in charge; Selby was the only intermediate station where this train stopped but it was still regarded as a local. (left) Selby's Up platform is bathed in sunshine on 11th August 1951 as a lone spotter' takes advantage of the facilities beneath the station name board. The 0-4-4T featured overleaf has now had a repaint and another change of identity (18th September to 14th October 1950 at Darlington), albeit a subtle one. So, having travelled some 175 miles thus far, we can take a rest at this crossroads prior to working on through Chaloner's Whin and York for the next stage of our northbound journey along the East Coast Main Line. *C.J.B.Sanderson.*